The Sleeve Waves

The Felix Pollak Prize in Poetry

The University of Wisconsin Press

The Sleeve Waves
ANGELA SORBY

The University of Wisconsin Press
1930 Monroe Street, 3rd Floor
Madison, Wisconsin 53711-2059
uwpress.wisc.edu

3 Henrietta Street
London WC2E 8LU, England
eurospanbookstore.com

Printed in the United States of America

Library of Congress Cataloging-in-Publication Data

Sorby, Angela, author.
  [Poems. Selections]
  The sleeve waves / Angela Sorby.
      pages   cm — (The Felix Pollak prize in poetry)
  ISBN 978-0-299-29964-4 (pbk. : alk. paper) — ISBN 978-0-299-29963-7
(e-book)
  I. Title. II. Series: Felix Pollak prize in poetry (Series).
  PS3619.O73A6   2014
811'.6—dc23
                                        2013027994

In memory of Professor Nelson Bentley, 1918–90

Oaks and garrets lit the falling dusk.

Contents

Acknowledgments   ix

I
Night Vision   3
Fallout   5
What Might Happen Might Not   6
Hard Bop   7
The Knit   9
Kochanski's, Saturday Night   11
Stopping at the Joyce Kilmer Rest Area on a
    Snowy Evening   12
The Disappearances   13
Trance Music   14
Spill   15
Golden Spike   16
Close Shave   18
The Ghost of Meter   20
Petition   21
Wide Boulevard, Tiny Apartment   22
Boom Town   23
Blood Relative   25
Letter to Hugo from the Land of the Living   26
End of the Century   27
Nonsense   28
Flatland   29
Double Neighbor   31
Errand   33
Interstate   34
The Obstruction   36
Duct Tape   38

II
Pastoral   41

III

Thrifting   45

Paradise, Wisconsin   46

A Is for Air   48

Duck/Rabbit   50

Notes from a Northern State   51

A Walk across the Ice   53

The Thorne Rooms   55

Just Looking   56

Blush   57

Thirst   58

Watson and the Shark   60

The Schoolteachers   61

Ink   62

Doppelzüngig   63

Fall Forward, Spring Back   64

Fat   66

Sacred Grove   68

Go-Between   70

Sofia's Stove   72

The Second Daguerreotype   73

Epistle   75

The Suburban Mysteries   76

The Sleeve Waves   77

Sivka-Burka   78

Acknowledgments

Heartfelt alphabetical-order thanks to those who provided collegial, familial, moral, and/or material support during the writing of this book: Vic and Jan Anderson, Faith Barrett, Jenny Benjamin, the Council for Wisconsin Writers, Matthew Cosby, the Edenfred Foundation, the Fulbright Scholar Program, C.J. Hribal, Catherine Hubbard, Jesse Lee Kercheval, David Kirby, Sandra Lee Kleppe, Maureen McLane, Monica Maniaci, Carla Marolt, Sheila McMahon (and everyone at UW Press), Naomi Shihab Nye, Liana Odrcic, Kris Ratcliffe (and all of my colleagues at Marquette University), Chris Roth, Francesca Roth, Ivan Roth, Jonah Roth, Melissa Schoeffel, Janet and Evan Sorby, Sarah Wadsworth, Ron Wallace, Larry Watson, and Adrianne Wojcik.

Thanks to the editors of the following journals, where versions of some of these poems first appeared:

Babel Fruit ("Letter to Hugo from the Land of the Living")

Barrow Street ("Paradise, Wisconsin")

Jacket ("The Suburban Mysteries")

Massachusetts Review ("Thrifting")

North American Review ("Stopping at the Joyce Kilmer Rest Area on a Snowy Evening")

Poets for Living Waters ("Spill")

Prairie Schooner ("Sivka-Burka," "Interstate," "Notes from a Northern State," "A Is for Air")

Superstition Review ("Ink," A Walk across the Ice," "Golden Spike")

Verse Wisconsin ("Kochanski's, Saturday Night," "Petition," in a different form)

Zone 3 ("Wide Boulevard, Tiny Apartment," "Fallout")

The line on the dedication page is taken from "Villanelle," by Nelson Bentley.

I

A wave is a disturbance that moves through a medium.
—Robert L. Weber, *Physics for Science and Engineering*

Night Vision

Changsa, 2011

Hunanese babies
wear tiger slippers
to ward off evil,
        though of course they're stronger
than their tiger-protectors,
and more rigorous,
and blunter,
and they know how to roar. Roaring's key:
it drowns out the philosophers
who drag the river
for texts

but miss
what's hidden deep
in baskets tied to the backs
of women selling fish
or sweeping streets:
babies who nap all day,
then open their eyes at night.
Living speakers can't remember
what it's like to be wordless,

if it's dull, divine, or both,

like the hundred-odd miniature
Buddhas stuffed
into one cave at Nanputuo.
The monk who wipes them with a rag
survived two famines
and a half-hanging
during the Cultural Revolution,
which thinned his hair

and did something to his ears:
now when the small gods wake in their velvety
toes and soles, he listens.

Fallout

Party at the beach,
but J refuses to go
because he can't swim.
11 years old. All day
I watch his cuteness
break open and fall away.
He finds Etta James
on YouTube and says,
"When I'm sad, only sad
songs make me better."
Already a needle
in his heart knows
how to find the chords
for all he's missing:
direct sunlight, easy listening.
Already the wax
cylinder's spinning
its old technology of longing,
and I recognize the boys I knew
in the '80s and '90s,
who dragged me to Fallout Records
so they could "look for something."
What? It has no name, this sadness
that feels like happiness.

What Might Happen Might Not

The psychic oboist charges
ten bucks per fortune.
He lodges above Clarke's Shoes
in Marinette, Wisconsin.
He says he doesn't know

how he sees what he sees.
He calls himself a *cleanser,*
a *healer*—of widows, of adoptees.
On slow days he sometimes
pauses between futures

long enough to play
Tomaso Albinoni's Opus 7,
blowing its pure notes virtuously,
as if they could filter
trash from the Menominee River,

but his oboe knows better—
it floats downstream keening.
Music is beauty consuming
itself. It is loss writ large,
it is an empty factory,

it is night come to clog
the Midwestern heart of the nation,
where the Green Bay Packers
tense and disperse
in random formations.

Hard Bop

The guy at the piano dump
pitches pianos, using a huge
claw to grab—lift—release.
Wippens, hammers, and jacks
scatter. A few wires snap,
and the rest snarl into silence,

the same silence
                    that snarls girls
who refuse to practice scales,
who sit hunched on the bench
reading *Secret of the Old Clock*

while the timer, set to one hour,
ticks backward. *You'll regret this*,
warn their mothers,

but the girls think the future
is in speeding convertibles,
like Nancy Drew's roadster,
or Chitty Chitty Bang Bang:
top up, top down, wheels retracted,
wings out, over the cliff into the ocean,
and boom—it's a boat.
                        They sense

what the dump guy knows:
to draw near the rim of the piano
pit is to witness

the body turn,
the hinge convert,

which is why the dump guy chains
a big ring of keys
outside his pocket.
Most open known doors, but a few,
he's not sure what they're for.
Those are his favorites.

The Knit

Honeyboy Edwards,
onstage at 93,

could be my Grandpa Harold's twin brother,
which makes no sense

since one's a live blues singer
and one's a dead Swedish American

asphalt worker,
but Grandpa, cool and silky

into his 90s,
dressed urban smooth,

and if a car hood was open,
no matter whose car,

he stuck his head in,
partly to suss out the engine,

and partly to spark a long
long conversation.

Can loud plaids cross the color line?
Can certain polyesters travel

beyond our peculiar national evil?
God knows nothing's simple,

but if one shirt could pass
between two strangers,

one living, one dead,
one black, one white,

Honeyboy Edwards is sporting
that shirt tonight. Its double-

knit gleams, so slick,
so inorganic,

it will outlast our muscle memory
of the twentieth century—

how it felt to sweat
under that fabric,

how plastered
against the skin a shirt

could turn timeless.
Unwrinkled. Ecstatic.

Kochanski's, Saturday Night

One more going-away
bash for a friend,
Afghanistan-bound, and the last thing
he wants is to hear some
peacenik strum. So up I shut,
and stick to seltzer,
as snowflakes fall with neutral

nonchalance

outside the bar. No windows.
Snow's too soft to cut
the chill, too gentle to kill
the one-armed drunk guy's engine.
Off he roars.
Oh, Lord.
To say the whole army
is stupid and wrong
is stupid and wrong, surely.
Walt Whitman thought he could heal
amputees with poetry. All I know
is when to leave a party.

Stopping at the Joyce Kilmer Rest Area
on a Snowy Evening

The whole East Coast is buried
in weather we manufactured
indirectly: the carbon-emissions unconscious.
How curious, this sameness.

Kilmer died fighting in France
in 1918. He wrote, "I think that I shall never see
a poem lovely as a tree,"
but was silent on the topic

of rest stops,
how the engine pauses,
and the Starbucks steamer hisses,
and all states feel equidistant

though this is nominally
New Jersey. He exploded
before he could picture a cup of coffee,
dark and complex

like modern poetry (Ezra Pound's maybe)
which, though stronger than Kilmer's,
still isn't cool and stark and pure
as a tree.

Soldier, soldier:
can you tell us where to go
now that we've shaken up the glass
globe and brought down the snow?

The Disappearances

The cold is large and pale and everywhere,
and falling on the South Milwaukee trees.
A cardinal moves his heat across the air,
above the clearance sales, the vacancies,
above the locks that fasten as they freeze
key-holders in the act of passing through.
A mortgage is a number no one sees:
a sleight-of-moon, a slip, a coming-due
of obligations tightening the screw.

The neighbor takes her name off every list,
and blows a fog onto the windowpane
to stamp a phony footprint with her fist.
Petite and singular, the print remains,
as if the neighbor walked out of her veins,
and up the glass—and up, and out of sight.
The cold invades the outlets, cracks, and drains.
The cardinal sheds its red coat overnight.
No blood runs deep enough to crack the ice.

Trance Music

Gerund comes from the Latin gerere *(future p. p.* gerundus*)*
to carry on; it carries on the power or function of the verb.
　—JOHN W. WILKINSON, 1895

Do you have 5, 10, 20
thousand dollars in credit card debt?
1-800-398-2067.
Call now! Imagine

                    walk-

ing the green spring
like a fawn sprung
from its spots.
No need to winter over.
You are the gerund.
The sky aches blue—
no cure, no analgesic.
Your debt is buried
like the skeleton
of a twin born dead.
Your feet trot horn-
hard, so far from human
you can't remember
how the voices sounded,
or what they wanted.

Spill

First I thought it was my furnace:
a black metallic odor
seeping through the glass-block
window into the yard.
Then I guessed it started
under my car: a shimmery river
of darkness. Then I figured: my lawn-
mower. Did it blow a plug?
What was that weird smell?
Where were the plovers, the sparrows,
the terns? My eco-neighbor,
out watering compost worms,
said, "It's BP!"

And then I knew.

It's not BP. It's him. It's me.
We've been gushing bullshit
since Earth Day, 1970.
What to do? Make a *poem*?

Christ.

Rilke beat everyone to it.
He wrote, "You must change your life."

Golden Spike

i.
To cure insomnia,
don't try. Pretend
the bed's a bunk
in a Pullman car,
bolted to the floor,
but moving steadily
from A to B.
The trick's to picture
neither A nor B
but the space
between characters,
large and yet limited,
like time—
how it elapses
everywhere at once,
despite the zones
fixed by railway
executives in 1883.
Wrong clock,
thought the Chinese
laborers who ached
but could not write.
The pain spread
from their arms
into their spines.

ii.
All the smart transcontinental titans know

vision is motion. To be
is not to be, but to go.
A koan: *keeping moving.*
An hour lost in Maine
is lost in California.

Close Shave

The perennials flash their steam-
punk violet hues,
daring human

women to lose

the flats, the control-
top hose. My mother
always says, "If I have a stroke,
don't let the hairs on my chin grow."
No clots yet: our spines

climb up to our minds,
node after node,
though lately the ladder
seems long, and the sky

is comatose
in the bird bath,
its whole weight
half-floating, half-drowning.
How strange, murmur the bearded

irises, *how entrancing,*
to drop petals into the dirt.
Slowly they cede
their beauty,

except on posters
in suburban kitchens
where Van Gogh's irises press
predictably against the wind,
as if color were muscle,

as if it were possible to resist
the copyists, the corset-makers, the stylized
forces of nature. Tonight I'll pull
on my scuffed black boots,
where there's space
to stash a razor.

The Ghost of Meter

1.
"The fault lies with an over-human God,"
wrote Wallace Stevens (bless his brittle heart).
His balding broker's head began to nod,
then, Humpty-over-Dumpty, broke apart,
all smash and scatteration. There's an art
to making chickens hatch. His spacious mind
compelled him to consume the yellow part
for salt. His daughter knew: he could not find
the words to leave ought but his words behind.

2.
Our father, Wallace Stevens, you are blind
to all we see. We walk you in our arms
like corpse-walkers in China, poised behind
the body, passing factories and farms
en route to the home province. No alarm
can jolt you from your sleep. The black-eyed girls
who pass on bicycles are swift and warm,
and as they ride the road they need unfurls
as if there were no fathers in the world.

Petition

I don't want to pay
all the parking tickets my junkie
handyman racked up
using my Honda

while I was in Asia
on a Fulbright fellowship,
but hey! The judge says his wife
also did a Fulbright,

"had a fantastic time,"
and packed her white
privilege as a carry-on.
It was oversized. The airline

didn't charge her a dime.
The judge declares
all fees dismissed,
but it takes me awhile

to find the exit,
because there are two elevators:
one for courthouse clients,
and one for prisoners.

Wide Boulevard, Tiny Apartment

At night Seattle's scenery
sinks into Elliott Bay.
No toga party, no everybody limbo! No.
Limbo is stalling on the floating
bridge. Limbo is look out a cop.
Limbo is the Frontier Room's closed—
even that guy Ben with scars for a chest
went home. A young woman lives
with a man she doesn't love:
this is deep structural corruption,

the way the Pacific Ocean
keeps acting like an ocean,
even in dead zones
where toxins are man-made:
PS oligomer, bisphenol A.

So why does the brain bother
to rebuild itself in sleep
(carefully, nerdily)
as the blacked-out woman
dreams of drunk-

driving off a bluff?
O but they love her,
these organs she shreds:
gently the pons and the meek cerebellum
follow her to bed.

Boom Town

Raven scours the Pike
Place Market. He's bereft:
the sun he once kept

in a cedar box is lost,
"replaced by an exact replica,"
as his brother the human

junk-picker mutters,
combing a dumpster
for cans. In the version of history

that didn't happen,
everyone's Salish,
Makah, or Tsimshian,

and under the Sound
a squid the size of Vashon
spurts ink enough to blot

out the Constitution,
but in lieu of that, *what?*
Sales stalls. Hipsters. Blind

buskers by the pig sculpture,
bending notes with a slide.
The singer bangs a crate.

The ground vibrates.
There is a fault,
a fault under Seattle,

from Fall City to Whidbey,
not *fault* as in guilty,
but *fault* as in geology,

bigger and deeper
than any historical error,
which is why Seattle can't gentrify,

not entirely,
no matter how tightly
the newcomers close their eyes,

no matter how hard they visualize
a PDF copy, not dirty,
not bloody, as if the Coast

were not the West,
as if some app could elevate
the city above the quake.

Blood Relative

When my grandmother
was cremated she relaxed
enough to dissolve
off the Pacific shelf,

but alive she moved
neck-deep in nerves,
the way a spiny dogfish swims
even when it slumbers,

picking up electromagnetic
fields from the sea.
She'd disappear
to jump off the Aurora bridge,

and though she never did,
I still sense her slow surreal
fall in my chest. She always said
Light up to make the bus come,

which makes me miss smoking,
how it fills the lungs
with poison
that feels like heaven:

one suck on a Winston
will draw the Ballard #10,
its driver seeking
fire in the fog.

Letter to Hugo from the Land of the Living

Flew through White Center in a borrowed Volvo.
White Center, where they tried to snuff your ghost.
They used a tin can. They didn't know who the hell you were
but they knew how it smells to suffer. Still you drift.
Excuse me while I block your path. Your eyes glide past,
seeking a type of female English major (younger, prettier)
who doesn't exist anymore. The current crop would sue your ass.
So listen: *soul retrieval.* I know, it's crap—a New Age metaphor,
so let's call it *fishing. Fishing from the hood of an old car*
as bait floats down the Skagit. You're parked at the edge,
waiting to yank—what—salmon? No, too heavy. Yuck:
in the Northwest (until recently) souls weren't sexy.
This one's moldy and mossy. Light rain falls on the scene
like a net. You can't start a fire with wet wood. In this state,
no one freezes to death. They rot. Look: the soul walks,
like a deer under the overpass as if its legs were barely up
to the task. Drunk, fat, and dead: only the latter lasts.
You must remember this: matter persists. Beer
still resembles beer when it's piss. Fresh water turns
to salt at Deception Pass. Richard—Dick—your shadow
can't be cast. Instead, clouds cover the mountains.

End of the Century

Chris "Slats" Harvey, d. 2009

1.
Post-millennium,
post-Lou Reed,
post-Elliott Smith,
it's too late to subsist
on three chords
and a leather jacket,
so your corpse looks tiny now,
floating out to sea,
much tinier than a human soul
ought to be.

The waves move autoerotically
because they don't give a damn

2.
about us velveteen rabbits.
We thought we could make ourselves real
by knowing the words to songs.

Nonsense

Colorless green
ideas sleep furiously,
but hang it all, Noam Chomsky,
you can't drain meaning out,

not entirely,

because say you have a sealed can of Diet Coke
in your messenger bag
(not that you are a messenger)
and it's dented and the dent
weakens the aluminum so it leaks all over,

then still, dammit: wet
Kleenexes and a wet wallet.

That dream *you failed a math class*
and now you have to retake it at the age of forty
but you can't find the classroom
and you're in your pajamas,
even that means

and keeps on meaning,
which is not the same as thinking:
it's an outside pressure,
a chemical insoluble in water,

as is evident when the moon crinkles
Lake Michigan so it shimmers
like a black plastic Glad bag
but bigger, and inside
there's more stuff (not all of it trash)
than any one sleeper remembers.

Flatland

At 46 I climb
the Cascade Mountains of my mind,
which is easier on the knees
than physical climbing,
but harder than dreaming,

since every step reminds me
I'm far from childhood,
far from the State of Washington,
"in a dark wood," in midlife,
like Dante, only Unitarian,

and therefore stripped of all faiths equally

as I walk two pugs
through a nun cemetery
behind the boarded-up
Archdiocese of Milwaukee.

The nuns recuse themselves:
they don't care whose sacred
text was right,

and I'm edging closer
to their neutrality,
which is a hum in the trees,
mingled with crickets,
but firm enough to ease
all opinions, even righteous ones,
off like a habit shed.

The Virgin bows her head:
she's plastic, presiding
in a blue molded gown

over a shrine strewn with flowers.
She'll never biodegrade—
she's eternal as a juice box straw,
which makes me thirsty

for what she can't give me:
salvation, an abstraction
that flooded my limbs
in eighth grade
when I converted, briefly,
to a Christianity
that promised to carry
the girls' cross country team to victory.
We stood in a circle, praying
so fervently the field rose,
though the team lost State.

Now we're close
to sea level—
Mary, the dead nuns, and me,
and my phalanges are collapsing
into crooked bouquets,

so when paleontologists
dig up my bones, they'll wonder,
What was the ritual?
Who were the priestesses?
Where was their grove?
I want to leave them a note:

walk the dogs.
Let the oracles keep their secrets.

Double Neighbor

When I tire of unclear people,
their skin matte, their retinas black
as raccoon-masks, their vocabulary dense
with grit and fog,

I think, but what if they were clear?

We are not clear, you and I.
We are not vases, not lenses, not directions given
        to a rapt class on the first day of kindergarten.
We are not rainwater: look, when the deer come up
to drink from the bird bath, their tongues
cloud it up, but cloudy

is a subset of velvety
Canadian whiskey,
a dram to calm
the lees of the day, a way to relax
into the dirty easy

chair on the porch. The sun sets,
and our unclear neighbor
drives up with a grocery bag full
of God-knows-what,

but there's no God,
so her mysteries are intact. She's 95 and still
all we know is her name,
Mary, a name she carries lightly,
in common with thousands of others.
Mary: the word tells us nothing about her,
but what word would?
                Our lawns adjoin,
and the deer use all

the back yards on this street as one long hall leading
through this, our present tense—

our strange, indivisible evening.

Errand

The star and the star's child
      are both stars,
as is the star's child's child—
      the universe goes on and on,
which is not news, but gossip.
      No one can substantiate
such sweep. Walk the enormity
      with me, son, but let's not forget
the grocery list, *milk, rice, sugar,*
      because matter consumes
its way greedily into eternity,
      the pug with its large eyes,
the rust on the dry-docked boat,
      and the clouds—
            how they drink rain,
                and are rain.

Interstate

Is it because I am finally old
that my young body passes by?

I catch it in the corner of my eye.
It has no clear gender.

Its shoes are in its hand.
It is condemned to wander

the lots where truckers park
their big rigs. Wheels are taller

here. Drivers log fake
numbers in their books

to make long hauls last longer.

And on the dark shoulder,
a stranger: that body. Its skin

fits too tightly. Its face
is drawn,
        more notion than person,

like a pencil sketch of nightfall
fallen. Don't look back,

wheezes Bob Dylan,
on the radio between stations—

that body's heart is not your heart,
and all its cells are dead.

But Officer, I'm wide awake, I swear.
Go ahead. Slap my face. Pull my hair.

The Obstruction

Xiamen, PRC.
A bare apartment.
We speak no Chinese,
so what can we do
if our middle son eats
a fish head that sticks
in his throat?

When he breathes,
the bone breathes:
a sharp out and in,
more gill than lung,
more scale than skin.
We feed him hunks

of bread, hoping fiber
will force out the head.
Go, fish, go, we urge,
       until, at last: **goodbye.**
Later, we burn amber
incense on the porch

and watch the fish's
spirit leave our lives
in a curl of smoke—
still flexible and strong,
like the old monks
in Speedos who swim
out to sea at dawn.

Celibacy keeps us fit,
they say. To love
is to cede power.
At birth the infant
is helpless,
but so is the mother.

Duct Tape

To make the soul solid:
a Hohner harmonica.

Breathe out chords
and slowly it grows
sweaty and warm.

How many roads . . . ?

When the screws fall out
it's fixable, unlike children born
with normal skin,
the kind that age thins.

At airports harmonicas
rattle security.
The X-ray tech asks
Why so many holes?
What is it?
Will it explode?

Duct tape can keep
an old harp together,
and keeping's not nothing—
it's the opposite of terror:

fixed notes,
sticky integrity.
Steady now, breathes the B-flat
Hohner. *Hold me.*

II

The sheep, too, stand around—they think no shame of us,
and think you no shame of the flock, heavenly poet;
even fair Adonis fed sheep beside the streams.
—Virgil, *Ecologues*, trans. H. Rushton Fairclough

Pastoral

We're sheep. We knit
unitards no thief can lift.
We're exacting, but effortless.
We got a gig!
      —playing ourselves
      in an amphitheater so vast
      our fans disappear in the grass.
      Are they human?
      Are they Gods?
      We don't give a rat's ass.
We're *sheep:* our job
      is to stabilize the field.
We're purely instrumental.
We don't speak. Why bother?
In summer it's summer forever.

III

If light and gravity are waves, then what is waving?
—Xiao-Gang Wen, "Microscopic Origin of Gravity and Light"

Thrifting

Goodwill smells of sweat and whiskey. Still the tightwad
palms her penny. Nothing can escape
her grip. She does not wish

to be rich, only safe,
which is a way of backing slowly
into an unbuttoned cardigan sweater,

like Mr. Rogers (R.I.P.),
whose words were parsimonious,
as if he had no rage, no urge, no penis.

Yet Fred was as masculine—in his way—
as Abe, whose head the shopper holds
hard in her hand

until it marks her skin: a red ring with no tail,
its beginnings fused to its ends,
impossible to keep,

impossible to spend.
The cost of the loafers is unclear black
marker scrawled on black leather.

O Fred, your name means peace in the tongues of the ancestors—
so why these needs, these expenditures?
Peace suspended, peace-in-amber—
won't you be my neighbor?

Paradise, Wisconsin

Mary Nohl's house
is hemmed in by flora

and fauna she fashioned
from hand-mixed cement.

For years she practiced
the art of continuous error,

wrong turns taken
so meticulously

they began to form peonies,
horses, and trolls,

all cracked and lumpy.
Now the vandal's task

is obscure: to ruin ruins,
to spray-paint stones

that take gang tags
so easily even such small

crimes feel impossible,
like flying. And yes,

the cranes come too,
down from Baraboo

to shit all over.
When they spread

their white wings they fail
to resemble angels—

they're too saurian, too clumsy,
but as they rise

in the summer dark
they knock loose

the abstract idea of heaven,
and leave it behind,

like a thug's tooth,
in Mary's concrete garden.

A Is for Air

i.
Dismantle the desks.
Melt the monkey bars.
Rip the clock off the wall.
Augment the drinking fountain with fake
        marble cupids and replace

childhood with something easier,
say, lilacs afloat in their own scent,

and then,

then I can go back to Fernwood School
with my daughter and explain
that school is impossible
but worth the pain
because you learn an alphabet that settles

        into marvels, into fearless Jane
Eyre, whose childhood was miserable,
and whose face was plain.

ii.
Except my daughter is beautiful,
and she hates long novels,
and she's adopted from a country
with so many intimate Gods
that when I watch her I wonder
whose supernatural hands
are guiding her—
but of course it's just me,
bringing her a lilac
in a coke-bottle vase,
which she accepts,

because she wants to be polite,
as she steps gracefully over her p's and q's
into her lace-up flying leather

miraculous

cheerleading shoes.

Duck/Rabbit

What can be shown, cannot be said.
    —LUDWIG WITTGENSTEIN

It's a law:
even the same socks
aren't the same,
post-wash.

I cover the bed with singles,
some familiar, some strange.
Green stripes, peace signs,
and of course whites,
that are, like white people,
not really white,

which was Wittgenstein's point:
nothing matches.

Notes from a Northern State

We moved for jobs
to the land of dead
deer strapped to cars.
Deer country sure
ain't horse country—
no one rides anyone's back.

It's all fleeting sightings:
a flash of fur, a horn, a single
eye among the branches.
Tiny ice-fishing houses
dot the lakes, and in each house,
a man, a thermos,

and a phone with no reception.
Can't call the men.
Can't ask them how to gut
fish, or smoke venison.
Our mantle's antler rack
is ironic, from an L.A. thrift

store, hung with bits
of broken chandelier,
but it's grown grave
in Wisconsin, a state
that's neither boot-
nor mitten-shaped,

but larger and harder
to place: rivers pour
themselves into stillness.
Jesus preached "have faith"
at Galilee, but here every lake
is walkable in winter.

O Lord, we will always be strangers.

A Walk across the Ice

During the sea blizzards
she had her
own portrait painted.
　　—ANN SEXTON, "The Double Image"

Winter's what we're walking into. Our veins
map blue highways,
routes first traced
by William Least Heat Moon
in a travelogue my mother read me
years ago, before I could read myself,

before I wondered if Persephone
blamed her mother
for dragging her home by the braids.
Controlling bitch. But

winter's what we're walking into.
If I put my arm in her arm,
will it sink too far
into the interior,
like a bone spur,
or a stent?

It's late. The light is brief.
If her boots leak, mine fit her,

and so we walk into winter.
　　　　Our shared DNA
makes us too unstable for skates,
but there is a gliding,
a set of parallel tracks,

an ease,

because we did not take the cocker
spaniel with her large
infected ears—

because our postmenopausal bones
are light and porous—

and because the lake ice
is thick enough for a Zamboni,
so I can't fall through,
and she can't rescue me.

The Thorne Rooms

Art Institute of Chicago

We move like clumsy
poltergeists—too wide for the doors,
too big for the chairs.
We can only stare
as the rooms progress
through ages of teensy
domestic fashions:
Tudor, Victorian, Modern.

O for a beaker fit for a finch!
O for a pocket-divan!
How we burn to enter

the one-twelfth-scale kitchen.
There must be a way to smuggle food in—
a snip of chive or a blueberry—
but no. Maybe when we're very old,

we'll lose the urge to stuff ourselves
into the miniature
Art Deco parlor
with its lamp stamped Tiffany,
or maybe desire's
what makes old ladies so skinny.
They wonder, *Are we wiry*
enough to slip in? Are we ready?
They know the key

to power is not bulk
but compression,
which is why grown women
love dollhouses.

Just Looking

for C.F.R.

Love is solid but also narrative,
so no matter how far the frame expands—

the frame with its gilt edges,
its fleur-de-lis, its stylized squirrels—

there's always an outside
that ought to be in:

junk DNA, random ancestors,
spoons, spackle, syllables,

so when I say *I love you* I mean
I love the parts I want to see,

which is why the frame
is integral to the picture,

even in the calmest Vermeer,
Woman in Blue Reading a Letter.

She's been pregnant since 1664,
but she's content to wait,

which is how it feels to stand still
in the pool of your natural light,

filling an hour with exactly that hour,
the way humans fill skin in pictures.

Blush

Eighth grade. Sex.
How it made us
antsy. Dizzy.
How it forced us
into ourselves,
all slick and sticky—

quivers shooting
through dirt, down
roots, up stems.
Sex. How it pressed
us into flowering.
So embarrassing—

but embarrassing
like the preacher on the bus.
Armpit stains. Buzz cut.
He starts reading
Genesis aloud:
in the beginning—

Everyone snickers,
but soon falls silent,
because yes,
                    it happened to us.
The darkness. The sword-bearing angel.
The garden. The flood.

Thirst

Milwaukee Public Museum, 2010

Part Bible, part bullshit—
but which is which?

That's the Dead Sea
Scrolls in a nut-

shell: none can tell
the aleph from the rip,

God from a census list.
Airlessly the population drifts,

a thousand years dead,
still stuck in bits

and pieces to the clay.
In lieu of God's right hand,

ossuaries hold knuckle-
bones turned to sand.

Prophets? They're easy to picture.
What's tougher is lovers:

how flexible they were—
touching in tents,

their flesh mostly water,
leaving no trace,

except in the fountain
between two doors marked

men and *women*.
Drink,

and the gnostic text begins
its exegesis: how the sea

is the scroll's twin,
but deeper. Press

a lever and upwell
the same identical molecules

the spirit hovered over,
in darkness,

in the beginning,
and here is the miracle:

we can drink them,
again and again.

We can be purified.
We can be sated.

Watson and the Shark

Baronet Watson's emblem
depicted his lost foot,
which was eaten by a shark
off the coast of Cuba in 1849.
When he fell into the ocean,

Watson was fourteen,
an orphan,
not yet a baronet, not yet the ex-
Lord Mayor of London.
In Copley's oil,

Watson and the Shark,
the boy Watson's long hair
streams like elegant
seaweed. He's nude. The shark
wants to consume

his luminous flesh,
but so does every viewer.
Together we hold Watson half-
underwater. He looks more like a girl
than a predator. The paint

suspends Watson
in pigment that makes us believe
there's a new world floating
behind the painting,
alive with edible leaves.

The Schoolteachers

When we visit the Gardner Museum
we never see Rembrandt's
Storm on the Sea of Galilee.
It's burgled. Only thieves
know where it rages—
so we repair to Whistler's Wand,

the Degas, and the Florentine credenza.
We can locate the Sea,
the earth's lowest,
in *McKnight's Geography*,
but Rembrandt's weather is out
of Doppler-radar reach,

gone like the students
we can't begin to teach.
They use prison shivs
to tattoo H-O-M-E-S-I-C-K
on their skin. They mix
ballpoint pen ink

with ash, and rub it in.
They think we're shocked.
They think we're "sivilized."
But we've stared down the blank
space on the wall:
no boat, no disciples, no Christ,

and when we die we'll come back
from Bardo as birds.
We'll light on the Gardner's roof
with our wings still warm,
and we'll offer ourselves
as interpreters of the storm.

Ink

Samuel Steward, d. 1993

The tattoo artist's
testicular tumor
came from a teratoma,
a malabsorbed embryonic twin.
The doctor said what mattered
was a cure.
The tattooist demurred:
what mattered to him
was the little sib lodged
in his right testis,
expanding benignly
at first, then deadly.

The teratoma took it slow.
Always the muffled music.
Always the black ink bath.
Always the guest in the guestroom

repeating

its fragments of DNA.
The tattooist covered
his calves with roses.
He wanted to send a single
stem to his twin,
but it couldn't be delivered
past the blood-brain barrier,
past the wall in the heart
that holds the possible
and the impossible
in adjoining cells,
but apart.

Doppelzüngig

In medieval allegories,
Death's like us, but smarter.
He covers his face

to block his rank
odor. Last night
a raccoon-corpse

flooded the yard.
No visible body,
just a scent so fishy

it plunged us
into a pre-human
anoxic ocean. We fought

to breathe.
Why didn't we go indoors?
Why did we sit

in deck chairs
letting it come—
this wave we couldn't begin

to grasp
with our tiny
opposable thumbs?

Fall Forward, Spring Back

Since I hate friendly
dogs they love me,
or maybe it's sincerity

that spooks me—I sniff
their eager scent
and get a hit so strong

it makes me dizzy.
Fall is complex:
part ochre, part setter.

The dog on the corner
isn't pure fur; his flesh
heats up as he barks.

I rush past to skirt
his to-do list.
       Still, he insists:
throw a stick, throw a stick,

as if I were not person but park,
a maze designed by Frederick Law Olmsted,
groves, curves, vistas,

and undergrowth "for mystery."
Olmsted said scenery
"unbends the mind,"

but what then? Unbent,
trees gather and store
the sun. Unbent, space grows

larger than any one thought, or feeling:
always this tossing,
always this retrieving.

Fat

It is not the look but the act
of overflowing that attracts:

this falling out of an XXL shirt,
over the edge of the Rascal

scooter at Piggly Wiggly,
this turning a corner

into the snack aisle,
bearing the impossible

burden of the body,
how fat folds conceal

a rib cage identical
to the cage inside

the U.S. president
since no one's exempt

from the urge
to enlarge into eternity,

like the heads at Mt. Rushmore,
or the Statue of Liberty,

to extend the self beyond
its airplane seat,

into the space of strangers,
into discomfiting touching,

to gorge on sleeve after sleeve
of cookies, each stamped

OREO, starting and ending
with the same letter *O,*

seductive and circular as the wheels
Ezekiel saw and instantly

craved so intensely
he thought they were part of his soul.

Sacred Grove

David Shields appears
on PBS to proclaim
the death of the novel,

but I always knew
the library was a repository
of corpses. By third

grade their silence
attracted: so pasty, so inky,
so compliantly unreal,

so unlike the reconstituted
orange juice smell
that took dominion

over us children,
recalling our obligation
to grow, to thrive, to speak.

The novel, bloodless
and cadaverous,
could keep secrets

grave-deep,
which is why it's tempting
to worship trees:

so many pages,
poised to leap,
like Daphne,

from sap to text—
the second-best kind
of little death.

Go-Between

i.
Just before it died,

their marriage went to Madeleine Island
with me, their third-wheel friend.
Why does beautiful weather
have no shame,
like a ukulele at an execution?

At dusk we drank at Tom's Burned-Down Café,
a tent stretched over ashes.
Was it a psilocybin flashback
that made me think I could coax them together,

like God if God were God?

We drained our pints.
The sun set, though I whispered *pause*—

Down, down it went,
metabolized by night.

ii.
Terrance McKenna, the ex-
hippie ethnobotanist,
says mushrooms
are the earth's way
of conversing with human brains,

but we are deaf,
made too sad by sadness, too joyful
by joy. Whatever the fungal shibboleth,

we're sitting here still
at Tom's Burned-Down Café,

missing everything.

Sofia's Stove

A nineteenth-century Norwegian stove,
tall and ornate, forces heat
through my friend's villa
in Hamar. It's hard to let
her have her stove,
because I've been cold
since 1979.
I want to screech *That stove*
is rightfully mine!
Still it sits in Norway
as winter enters the Western hemisphere
gently, like a sister,
through the unlatched door.

January spreads quickly,
the way life flattens into a broad field
of snow: we are old in our mittens.
Even our cats know.

Sofia, friend, I allow you your stove,
the one you earned
and deserve. Our fortunes curve inward
like our toenails—once supple,
now brittle. It's best to stand
a little apart from the fire.
The stove assembles itself,
not in real time but in the warm
intervals between women,
the place where we can't meet,
where strawberries redden and stay
impossibly sweet.

The Second Daguerreotype

of Emily Dickinson, Amherst College Library Special Collections, 2012

Her teacher,
Edward Hitchcock,
took plaster casts
of Amherst's dinosaur tracks,
but could not reconstruct
their musculature,
how they moved when Massachusetts
was steamy, newly broken
off Pangaea, and yet

in Dickinson's photo
a shape is visible under her dress:
not America,
but an older landmass,
its theropods killed by a comet,
flood, or volcano. Then
came the pressure
that turned organic matter
into coal. She clearly

knew an occult route back
to those astonished
condensed creatures
fueling her planetary
distribution: inky, glittery carbon
no longer exchanging
atoms with oxygen.
How strange, how alien

to be both an energy source
and a burner. She's not quite human
to us. We're not quite human

to her,
           but there are two women
in the picture. No wonder
she presses her hand
hard against Kate Scott Turner's
spine, as if to say *We were friends*
in real time, which matters more than poetry,
because it leaves no trace. The print
is not the finger. The paper
is not the face.

Epistle

Sylvia Plath, Bad Mom,
we love how you wet

no towels for us,
your readers. You turned on

the gas and let it run
into the vast unwholesome system

of English 101:
that's where we found you,

curled in the Norton,
and you said: Hello,

and we said: Mom.
How you hated that!

How un-sexy
to be Mom to so many

perfectly sane young
tattooed women wondering

Am I crazy?
Still you smiled

yourself blurry,
modeling swimwear

in the student paper,
giving us your all.

And we took it.

The Suburban Mysteries

after H.D.

Begonias lashed
to stakes still fall,
crushed by the weight

of storms so light
they travel miles
above the turf.

Damage is reason-
proof: a spine compresses
in a dream,

and the dream's daughter
can't walk it off.
She's shorter

by a fraction.
There are eyes
in the begonias,

eyes in the thunder,
eyes controlling
the children's limbic reactions.

Have you seen me?
O to stare from a milk carton,
gone through fields

too dark to farm,
into the old forest's old
dissolving arms.

The Sleeve Waves

The pigeon-catchers come out to catch—

wait for it—

yes—

pigeons. They use a net
& a rusty cat carrier.
A pigeon'll fetch
"three dollars on the open market,"
says the older catcher.
The younger catcher, with dyed black hair,
says nothing. He looks
like he thinks about pigeons
all day. His eyes have turned

                          white & grey,
& they've flown away.

Sivka-Burka

Sleep's smashed
to shards. Lap-
tops glow in bed after bed.
Strangers pull strangers
into their heads. And yet,
as starlings scatter,
unwired Russian grandmothers
strip to drink

what's left of the sun
after the death of Stalin,
and the collapse
of the Soviet Union.
No one pays attention
to these women but themselves,
as they harvest
vitamin D directly,

laying out a foil sheet
and roasting.
Slowly, they turn
tree-bark brown,
not to please their husbands,
but just to absorb
something profound
without reading.

The Felix Pollak Prize in Poetry
Ronald Wallace, General Editor

Now We're Getting Somewhere • David Clewell
Henry Taylor, Judge, 1994

The Legend of Light • Bob Hicok
Carolyn Kizer, Judge, 1995

Fragments in Us: Recent and Earlier Poems • Dennis Trudell
Philip Levine, Judge, 1996

Don't Explain • Betsy Sholl
Rita Dove, Judge, 1997

Mrs. Dumpty • Chana Bloch
Donald Hall, Judge, 1998

Liver • Charles Harper Webb
Robert Bly, Judge, 1999

Ejo: Poems, Rwanda, 1991–1994 • Derick Burleson
Alicia Ostriker, Judge, 2000

Borrowed Dress • Cathy Colman
Mark Doty, Judge, 2001

Ripe • Roy Jacobstein
Edward Hirsch, Judge, 2002

The Year We Studied Women • Bruce Snider
Kelly Cherry, Judge, 2003

A Sail to Great Island • Alan Feldman
Carl Dennis, Judge, 2004

Funny • Jennifer Michael Hecht
Billy Collins, Judge, 2005

Reunion • Fleda Brown
Linda Gregerson, Judge, 2007

The Royal Baker's Daughter • Barbara Goldberg
David St. John, Judge, 2008

Falling Brick Kills Local Man • Mark Kraushaar
Marilyn Nelson, Judge, 2009

The Lightning That Strikes the Neighbors' House • Nick Lantz
Robert Pinsky, Judge, 2010

Last Seen • Jacqueline Jones LaMon
Cornelius Eady, Judge, 2011

Voodoo Inverso • Mark Wagenaar
Jean Valentine, Judge, 2012

About Crows • Craig Blais
Terrance Hayes, 2013

The Sleeve Waves • Angela Sorby
Naomi Shihab Nye, Judge, 2014